so as us

And then we'll do a little bit of meditation to settle down our minds generate a positive motivation for what we're doing here tonight. So the prayers could be put up on the screen. And while reciting the prayers it's good if you can to imagine the buddha in front of you. And think that this image of the buddha represents all enlightened beings all buddhas. And all other objects of refuge all of your spiritual teachers. So all the positive qualities of the buddha dharma. And sangha embodied in this one figure of shakimuni buddha made of light pure transparent radiant. And really from the depths of your heart feel that you are taking refuge in the buddha his teachings the dharma. And the sangha those who are sincerely dedicating themselves to following these teachings following the path. And the reason for relying on the buddha dharma. And sangha is to be of benefit to others ourselves to transform ourselves into someone who can benefit others not harm them. And help them in their spiritual practice as well in whatever way is most skillful. And meaningful i go for refuge until i'm enlightened to the buddha the dharma. And the supreme assembly by my practice of giving. And other perfections may i become a buddha to benefit all sentient beings i go for refuge until i'm enlightened through the buddha the dharma. And the supreme assembly by my practice of giving. And other perfections may i become a buddha to benefit all sentient beings i go for refuge until i'm enlightened to the buddha the dharma. And the supreme assembly by my practice of giving. And other perfections may i become a buddha to benefit all sentient beings may all sentient beings have happiness. And causes of happiness may all sentient beings be free from suffering. And the causes of suffering may all sentient beings be inseparable from happiness that is free from suffering may all sentient beings abide in equanimity free from attachment for friends. And hatred for enemies reverently i prostrate with my body speech. And mind i present clouds of every type of offering actual. And imagined i declare all my negative actions accumulated since beginning this time. And rejoice in the merit of all holy. And ordinary beings please remain until the end of cyclic existence. And turn the wheel of dharma for living beings i dedicate my own merits. And those of all others enlightenment this ground anointed with perfume strewn with the flowers adorned with mount meru for countenance the sun. And the moon i imagine this as a butterfield. And offered may all living beings enjoy this pure land. And let's recite the mantra of the buddha seven times. And while reciting the mantra visualize light flowing from the buddha the light represents his qualities his wisdom compassion love. And all the other enlightened qualities. And imagine the light flowing into you. And completely filling your body. And mind. And it purifies all negative aspects of your body. And mind like negative karma afflictions as well as sickness any kind of physical problems imagine all of these getting purified. And the light also nourishes our positive qualities of positive potential our qualities like love. And compassion. And wisdom. And so on. So they can grow more. And more eventually becoming qualities of an enlightened mind [Music] is is [Music] me my. So [Music]. So really feel that the light from the buddha has completely purified your mind. And your body of all that is negative. And your mind is blessed to be able to attain all the positive qualities leading you to the state of enlightenment. And in the meantime enabling you to be of greater. And greater benefit to others. And to the world. And then just take a few more moments on your own to really make sure that your motivation for joining this class is an altruistic one if you are comfortable with bodhichitta the aspiration to become a fully enlightened buddha to be able to help all living beings. Then you can bring that into your mind recall that motivation. But if you're not yet sure if that's what you want to do. Or that you're able to do that. Then just generate whatever kind of altruistic attitude you're comfortable with feeling the wish to be of as much benefit to others other beings as possible in your life. And of course benefiting yourself as well because. When we engage in learning. And practicing the dharma we ourselves benefit it's just natural our mind becomes more calm. And peaceful more positive fewer disturbing thoughts. And emotions of course it takes time for that to happen it's not like an overnight instant change. But gradually over time we definitely see positive effects on ourselves in learning. And practicing the dharma. So really try to feel that wish to benefit yourselves. And as many other people. And beings as possible okay. So this is only the second class in this series of classes on the 70 topics. So last week i began by giving the background to this text what the 70 topics are all about. And how they are the main topics explained in the text by maitreya called ornament for clear realizations. Or abi samayalam one of the most important texts in the nalanda tradition the tradition of the great indian masters explaining the buddha's teachings. And so i gave some background to that text. And then an overview of the text which has eight chapters each chapter covering a different we're called category. Or also we could say clear realizations. So basically the text is explaining the bodhisattva's path what a bodhisattva needs to do mainly the kind of realizations they need to develop in their minds in order to progress on the path leading to full enlightenment buddhahood. And last week towards the end of the class i showed a chart of the five paths a path of accumulation path of preparation path of seeing path of meditation path of no more learning. So those are like the five stages that a bodhisattva goes through on their way to enlightenment. And. But also hearers. And solitary realizers have five paths five stages in their process of attaining nirvana. And one of the topics that comes up in talking about the five paths is the obscurations these are factors within our mind that need to be cleared away need to be eliminated in order to make progress on the path. And eventually reach our goal. And i wanted to give a bit more explanation tonight about these obscurations because the this the school that this text is explained according to is the yoga character mika school. And they have quite a unique way of explaining the obscurations. And also the paths of the three vehicles. So i want to explain that first. So whoever is putting up this slides if you could put those on the screen okay. So obscurations. And ysm stands for long name. So just to abbreviate it. So again there's two kinds of obscurations the first one is called afflictive obscurations. Or ao for short. And according to this school this mainly includes ignorance the ignorance that conceives of a self-sufficient substantially existent self. Or person. So this is a conception that everybody has it's inborn innate even animals. And insects. And babies any being that has a mind it isn't you know an enlightened being we all have this conception in our mind. So it's inborn innate. And [Music] it views our own self our own being. And believes that there is a certain type of self which has these qualities of self being self-sufficient substantially existent which is a mouthful of words. And probably doesn't make a lot of sense to you. But it's described as a sense of an i a me that seems to be like someone in charge like a boss. Or a ruler a ceo okay. So there seems to be an eye somewhere inside of us that owns our body. And mind it's like the owner of the body. And the mind. And also controller controls our body. And mind controls our life. And our actions. So that sense of a of a controlling eye. Or ego if you want to call it that's the meaning of this conception. And it's a type of ignorance. So that's the main afflictive obscuration. And the afflictive observations are the ones that keep us in samsara. And prevent us from getting free of samsara. And attaining nirvana liberation. So this is the main thing that binds us to the wheel of life having to die. And be reborn again. And again. And again. And so that's the main thing that needs to be overcome to be eliminated in order to be free of samsara. And in addition to that there are other afflictions like anger attachment jealousy pride. And so forth that arise from this ignorance as well as seeds. So the term seed you shouldn't think of it like a physical seed like a barley seed. Or a tomato seed that will grow into a plant it's not something physical it's something subtle that is left in our mind. When we have states of afflictions. When we get angry for example. Or ignorance you know. When ignorance manifests in our mind it leaves a seed it plants a seed in our mind that will give rise to another experience of the same type later on. So in addition to getting rid of ignorance. And the other afflictions we also have to get rid of the seeds. So those afflictive states of mind don't grow anymore. So those are the afflictive obscurations. And then there's the second kind of observation are called knowledge obscurations other translations are obscurations to omniscience. Or some translated as cognitive obscurations. So kos for short okay. So this school says there are two kinds of knowledge obscurations there's of course one. And a subtle one. So the course one is the conception of subject. And object being of different natures. Or entities along with its seeds. So this conception i just the book a little bit last week about how this school is similar to cheetah matra. Or mind only school because they believe that there are no external objects external objects means objects that we perceive that are that it exist out there separate from our mind independent of our mind that's how things appear to us that's how things seem to be. But that's wrong that's an illusion. And in reality the objects that we perceive for example a flower. When we see a flower although the flower looks like it's sitting out there just waiting for us to come along. And see it. And smell it. And touch it. But the flower that appears to our visual consciousness. Or any of our consciousnesses actually comes from an imprint in our mind. Or a seed kind of like a seed. Or an imprint that's stored in our mind left from previous actions previous experiences. So what happens. When we see a flower is the seed ripens. And produces both the appearance of the flower as well as the consciousness like an eye consciousness that's perceiving the flower okay. So that's what actually happens with all the things that we perceive visual objects sounds smells taste. And so on. So everything we perceive is actually kind of a projection you might say of some seed in our mind.

And so the object like the flower. And the subject the mind that's perceiving it both of those two things arise together simultaneously from the same seed in the mind. And because the object. And subject arise together they are of one nature. Or one entity. And when it. When it said that two things are of this one nature. Or the same nature that means they arise together they abide together. And they cease together. And they can't be separated. So it doesn't mean they're the same they are two different things. But they have that kind of strong relationship of a rising together abiding together ceasing together. So for example with a flower. When we see a flower the flower that we see as well as the mind the subject seeing it are of the same nature. Or the same entity because they arise from the same cause the same seed. So that's the reality of things however ordinary beings don't realize that don't understand that. And instead we think that the object. And the subject perceiving it are completely separate. And cut off. And unrelated. And not of the same nature. So that's the meaning of this conception the conception of subject. And object being of different natures. Or different entities okay. So this is according to them of course obscuration to omniscience of course knowledge obscuration. Or cognitive obscuration. And also the seeds of that conception that are left in the mind. And then the the subtle knowledge obscurations are the conception of true existence along with its seeds okay. So this is a more subtle kind of wrong conception that sees things as truly existing. And a little bit later i will explain what this school means by true existence they reject. Or refute true existence they say true existence is false it's kind of funny to say it's true existence. But it's actually false it's wrong. But that's the term they use. And i will explain it a little bit later. But that they say that is the most subtle misconception that we have. Or wrong conception that we have that needs to be eliminated needs to be cleared away from our mind along with its seeds in order to for our mind to become a buddha's mind fully enlightened mind. And so those are the obscurations. And then down at the bottom it says there are both acquired acquired means learned like from our teachers. Or whatever like if you study a certain philosophical system that teaches these wrong conceptions. Then on top of the innate ones if there's an innate one you have additional ones that are acquired. And then innate innate. Or inborn that's what we are born with what we bring with us from past lives. So there's a there's an acquired. And an innate form of both of these obscurations afflictive observations. And knowledge obscurations. And i'm sure about that with regard to at least the subtle type of knowledge obscurations i didn't see any material about acquired forms of the course obscurations my guess is there probably are. But i'll try to find out for sure okay. So so uh. When a person is progressing along the path. When they reach the path of seeing the third path that's the point at which they attain a direct realization of selflessness. Or emptiness that's the time. When the acquired level of obscurations are eliminated. And they sort of they're all cleared away in one go. Then from. Then on one continues to meditate on selflessness. Or emptiness. And gradually eliminate the innate obscurations afflictive. And knowledge obscurations okay. So those are the obscurations. And then yeah. So just go back a minute. So prasan gika has a different explanation they don't have course knowledge obscurations they only have knowledge obscurations. And just in brief according to prasangika the afflictive obscurations are include mainly the conception of inherent existence believing there's an inherently existing i. And everyone. And everything else. So seeing all things all phenomena as inherently existing. So they say that's the main afflictive obscuration that needs to be eliminated in order to attain either nirvana. Or or enlightenment whatever it is you're trying to attain. So that means that to get out of samsara to free yourself from samsara it's not enough just to eliminate this more coarse type of ignorance about a self a self-sufficient substantially existent self. So we do have to overcome that one. But just by overcoming that one you will not be able to attain liberation from samsara you have to eliminate the deepest most subtle ignorance of inherent existence anyway. So that they're like i say there are differences in the different schools about would what are the observations that need to be eliminated in order to attain both liberation freedom from samsara as well as enlightenment. But yeah this this school has its own unique way of explaining the observations. And then the next slide shows another unique explanation of this school. And that is how practitioners of the three vehicles practice in order to attain their respective goals. So the three vehicles. So a vehicle the term vehicle if i remember correctly that itself refers to a state of mind a realization okay. So a vehicle is actually a realization. And so the first of the three vehicles is the hearers the vehicle of the hearers. And these are practitioners who listen to the buddhist teachings. And generate the wish to attain nirvana liberation freeing themselves from samsara. And so in order to attain their goal their main object of cultivation. Or meditation the main thing they meditate on is the subtle selflessness of persons. And that refers to the emptiness of a self-supporting substantially existent self. So again that's the sense of an i who's in charge the boss okay. So they meditate on the emptiness of that. And gain a realization of that kind of emptiness. And so that's what they meditate on that's their main object of meditation. And then the next column is the main object of abandonment. So what it is they are abandoning. Or eliminating is that conception that wrong conception of a self-supporting substantially existent self which again is afflictive the afflictive obscuration. So they're mainly trying to eliminate the afflictive obscurations because those are the things that keep us in samsara they have to be overcome to be free of samsara. And then the final the last column is what is their object of attainment. And they attain what's called here is enlightenment. So here is enlightenment that's the term used in the text. But it's it's nirvana a type of nirvana. Or liberation that hearers attain. And then

[Music] the the second vehicle is the vehicle of solitary realizers. So these are also practitioners who learn the buddhist teachings. And aspire to attain nirvana. But they have a somewhat different way of practicing. So their main object of cultivation. Or meditation here i put nonduality. And that means nonduality of subject. And object. So that's talking about this is the opposite of the conception that subject. And object are different entities. Or different natures okay. So we have that wrong conception thinking there's external objects. And objects. And perceivers are you know completely different. And unrelated. So there's that wrong conception. And they are trying to overcome that. So they meditate on nonduality meaning that subject. And object are not different entities they are one entity one nature. So that's their main object of meditation. And then their object of abandonment is the conception of duality conception of subject. And object being of different nature natures. Or different entities which is the course kind of knowledge obscuration okay. So that's going back to the previous slide the course level of the knowledge obscuration. So the solitary realizers overcome those eliminate those by meditating on nonduality. And as a result they attain a solitary realizer's enlightenment. So again it's nirvana. But a somewhat maybe more advanced type of nirvana than the hearers because they have eliminated a more subtle kind of obscuration in their mind the hearers have not. So the hearers don't eliminate that wrong conception of subject. And object being of different natures. And then the third type of practitioner the bodhisattvas this is the mahayana vehicle. And so their main object of cultivation. And meditation is emptiness of true existence. So that's the most subtle level of emptiness emptiness of true existence. And what they overcome. Or abandon their main object of abandonment is the conception of true existence seeing everything is truly existing. And again that's the subtle type of knowledge obscuration. So they abandoned that. But they also have to meditate on the other topics the other

topic topics of meditation they also have to meditate on the first one the hearers one subtle selflessness of persons they do meditate on that. And they eliminate the afflictive obscurations they also meditate on nonduality the solitary realizers object of meditation. And they eliminate the conception of duality the course knowledge obscurations. But their main practice is meditating on the emptiness of true existence. And realizing that realizing that kind of emptiness. And then they eliminate the subtle knowledge obscurations. And then the the the goal the final objective attainment is full complete enlightenment. Or buddhahood. So that's the enlightenment that the buddha himself achieved okay. So this is a little complicated. But it is
part of the study of the ornament. And yeah. When you go through the ornament this comes up again. And again how these three types of persons practitioners have three main objects of meditation that they meditate on as well as three different levels of objects that they are abandoning overcoming. And three different goals that

they attain. And there's also differences in the amount of time they spend on their path. So the hearers accumulate merit for it says around three lifetimes. Or more that's kind of the minimum. So they spend three lifetimes accumulating merit. And meditating on to cultivate their own type of wisdom in order to attain their goal here is enlightenment solitary realizers spend around 100 eons practicing accumulating merit. And meditating on their main objects of meditation in order to attain their goal of solitary realizers enlightenment. And bodhisattvas you've probably heard spend at least three countless great eons following their path accumulating merit. And developing their wisdom. And finally achieving full enlightenment buddhahood. And so because of the amount of time that is spent on the path the different practitioners will attain higher more superior levels of realization. And ability to be of benefit to others is any questions about this. So far the slide before this you have at the bottom nb what does that stand for oh i don't know what is it no to benny it's just a latin thing just take note of this [Laughter] is there any do you know of any distinction between the type of nirvana that heroes attain. And solo today realizes yeah they i mean it is said that they they do attain a a superior type of enlightenment. And i did look up some information. But i didn't have time to put it together today. So i can bring that up next time there are certain distinctions things that they are able to do that heroes are not able to do did you already say what their definition of true resistance is that's coming okay next slide [Laughter] okay. So the next slide next page okay. So. So again this term true existence may be used by different schools of tenants. But the way they understand it. Or explain it would be different. So according to this school the yoga character. So the first bullet point says the measure of true existence. So in in actual fact true existence doesn't exist it's actually a false mode of existence. And yet we do see things as if they were truly existing. So even though it doesn't exist it does appear to us we do see things as if they were truly existing. So what is that mode of existence that's called true existence. So this is kind of a technical explanation. Then i'll put it into simple words. So it's the existence of an object by way of its own uncommon mode of subsistence without being positive through the force of appearing to a non-defective awareness. So what that means is that two ordinary beings those who haven't realized emptiness everything appears as if it exists with its own uncommon. Or objective way of existing. So it seems to exist completely from its own side independent of the mind not depending at all on the mind. And even though this way of existing doesn't exist we do see things as as if that they existed that way because of this innate conception that's been in our mind from beginningless time it's always been there we've never been free of it. And so we've always seen things in this way. And most beings never question it they just go along with it buy into it. So the. Then the term non-defective awareness in there the end of that sentence. So it means it could be either a conceptual consciousness. Or a non-conceptual consciousness. So it could be conceptual. Or it could be like direct perception seeing hearing smelling tasting. And And so on. So just a consciousness that's not wrong. Or incorrect. So according to this school. And i think it's also true for the other type of svetantaka madhyamaka the sultanticus the way that things do exist for example a table probably all have tables nearby that we can look at. So the way the table exists is it the the conventional mode of existence there are two factors that need to be present. So one factor is that the object does have its own objective mode of existence you know there are certain features certain qualities in the object from the side of the object. But that's not enough just that alone isn't enough for the table to exist conventionally there needs to be something coming from the mind. So that mode of existence of the object the table has to appear to a mind a non-defective awareness okay not a wrong mind. But a correct mind. And then that mind will pause it. Or impute table on to the object. So those two things need to come together in order to say there is a table conventionally existing table. So one of my teachers said it's like two halves of an egg. Or two halves of a ball okay. So the two halves have to come together in order to make the hole something like that. So that's how things do exist conventionally. But if we were to think that the table has its own way of existing on its own completely independent of appearing to the mind. And being posited by the mind just totally from its own side that motive existing is false. And that's the meaning of true existence that's actually the meaning of true existence if we say the table is completely independent of the mind it has its own qualities features characteristics objective way of existing regardless of anybody's mind seeing it. And imputing it. And so on that's the meaning of true existence. And that kind of conception is the conception of permanence. Or absolutism. Or raiification there's different terms for that that's one of the two extremes extreme of permanence on the other hand if if one were to think that objects exist merely through the force of an awareness. And don't have their own uncommon objective mode of existence that's also incorrect that would be the extreme of nihilism. Or an annihilation. And so i think from their point of view what the prasan gigas are saying there's nothing in the object object the object doesn't have any characteristics. Or mode of existence from its own side objectively it's all just imputed by the mind posited by the mind. So this school would say that's nihilism you're falling into nihilism there has to be something coming from the side of the object otherwise the object is just non-existent. And a mirror mental construction. So so they say there's something from the side of the object something from the side of the mind those two things coming together make the conventional existence of the object. And so this way of explaining things according to them is how they avoid the two extremes the extreme of permanence on one hand the extreme of nihilism on the other. And so mainly in this text they use the term true existence. And down at the bottom the last bullet point has synonyms of true existence ultimate existence. And existence as its own reality. But i think the first two are the main ones that they use so. When this school is talking about the object of negation the object that needs to be negated to realize emptiness they use the term true existence. Or ultimate existence. But not inherent existence. So it's it's the prasangicas who use that term inherent existence. And have their unique way of explaining it. So you have to be careful which terms you use. And you know. When talking about this school you wouldn't say that their object of negation is inherent existence they do refute inherent existence on the ultimate level they say ultimately things don't have inherent existence. But conventionally they do. So they're actually a firm inherent existence on the conventional level. But refuted on the ultimate level. But from the prasangika point of view that's nuts [Music] you can't say that inherent existence exists conventionally. But not ultimately yeah. So they have their arguments about that. But anyway. So for this school better to use the terms true existence. And ultimate existence those are the things that they refute. And this is what it means to exist truly. Or ultimately any questions about that not that i'd be able to answer them. So they refute true existence conventionally no ultimately yeah ultimately this school yeah yeah this school no they refuted across the board. So both. So they refer to existence both conventionally. And ultimately yeah. And it's the inherent existence the inherent existence is what they don't refute conventionally conventionally yeah all these these different terms it can be quite a my other question yeah you know. So the yogurt chairs talk about the two subtle selfless two types of subtle selflessness of phenomena yeah do they also assert the second kind this school yeah i don't know i can't recall it coming up in the ornament it didn't i don't think it came up in the ornament. But that doesn't mean they don't it just might not may not be emphasized there's a book called study of tantrica by lopez donald donald lopez yeah. So he really goes into this photonic attendance in great depth in detail. So you might find it in there. But yeah i think in the ornament because it's you know the intended audience are bodhisattvas. And the main object of meditation for bodhisattvas is emptiness of true existence. So that's the one that's mainly mentioned in the ornament. But it's also not the most i mean it comes up again. And again. But not in the same way as in nagarjuna's texts. Or chandra kiri's text because the ornament is mainly talking about the method side of the path the the bodhisattva's path not. So much the wisdom side of the path. But it is definitely there okay. So yeah that's just kind of some more background information about this school. And then tonight i wanted to go into more detail with the first of the 70 topics. So again this is in chapter one chapter one is explaining the exalted knower of all aspects the first of the three exalted knowers. And that is another term for omniscient mind light mind buddhist mind. And then there are ten topics in chapter one. And like i said last week that's the biggest chapter in the book it's just full of wonderful information. And the

very first of the ten topics in
chapter one is it's called generated mind which is another term for bodhichitta. So you can go to the next slide. So generated mind is semkie in tibetan. And it's i'm kind of curious about where the term bodhichitta comes from because this text always uses that term generated mind semke instead of bodhichitta. So i haven't done extensive research research into this. But i just you know in the lam rim most of our studies like in the lam room. And lojong. And And so on they use the term budi cheetah however in this text which is meant to be the source for the long room they use this other term generated mind anyway. So the first verse of
chapter one gives a kind of i don't know if it's really a definition. But it's an explanation of what the generated mind is. So it's the words in red the generated mind is desire for perfect complete enlightenment for others welfare. And so that half of a verse is often quoted for example in la matsang kappas. And other other books as the you know source for

the explanation of of what is bodhichitta. So i'm going to kind of switch back. And forth sometimes i'll use the term bodhichitta sometimes i'll use the term generated mind. So just know that they're they're the same thing just different terms for them. And he uses the term desire which can be a little surprising because you know we tend to think of desire as something negative like an affliction like another term for attachment however the word desire isn't always negative it can be it's also used for example the desire for enlightenment. Or the desire for liberation okay. So it depends on what it is we have desire for if we desire a boyfriend. Or ice cream. Then you know that's a samsaric mind the desire for liberation desire for enlightenment is something positive. And constructive. And even though he uses the word desire it really refers to another mental factor that's usually translated is aspiration having aspiration. And so it said that there are two kinds of desires. Or aspirations that are necessary for bodhichitta to have this mind of bodhichitta the first is aspiration for others welfare. So that comes about by mainly cultivating compassion compassion is the most important factor leading to bodhichitta. So recognizing i mean first of course we have to recognize samsara our own samsara how we are stuck in this situation of being under the control of afflictions. And karma dying. And being reborn again. And again. And again having to go through all these painful experiences. And so on. So we have to understand samsara its faults its disadvantages. And generate this strong determination to get out of it to free ourselves from it. And then looking at others other sentient beings recognizing that they are stuck in samsara too they're in the same situation under the control of karma. And afflictions having to die. And reborn again. And again. And go through all these sufferings. So that gives rise to compassion you know this having the determination to be free of samsara for oneself is like it's like compassion for oneself self-compassion like somebody brought up last week. But. Then a bodhisattva will extend that to others. And realize they want to be free of suffering just as much as i do. And i want to help them. And in the process of developing bodhichitta you contemplate how others are have been kind to us one of the methods for generating bodhichitta involves thinking how everybody has been my mother. And my father buddha said that he himself said those words that everyone has been our mother. And our father as well as our child. And our brother. And our sister. And our friend. And all of our happiness all the [Music] needs. And pleasant experiences. And everything that we have comes from others. So without others we wouldn't we wouldn't be even be alive much less have any any enjoyments. And also for spiritual practice we need others as the objects the recipients of our spiritual practice to practice generosity ethics patience cultivate love kindness compassion. And so on. So one contemplates this dependence on others. Or interdependence with others plus how others are suffering in samsara. And this gives rise to a strong sense of compassion.

And the wish to help others. Or the aspiration for others welfare. So that's the first of the two types of aspiration. And that's said to be a causal aspiration that's the cause of bodhichitta okay. So that precedes bodhichitta. So we have to have this strong wish to relieve the suffering of others. And then look for how to do that how to fulfill that wish. And we come to realize that there's only one way to really help all sentient beings. And that is by becoming a buddha only a buddha a fully enlightened being has all the abilities the qualities whatever it takes to be able to help sentient beings become free of samsara. And help them attain nirvana. And enlightenment. And so on. So you know. When one needs to know very well the qualities of the buddha like the four buddha kayas. And all the other abilities that a buddha has. And then. And then you realize okay that's what i need to do in order to fulfill this wish to help others i need to become enlightened. So that's the second aspiration attaining perfect complete enlightenment in order to benefit others. So that second type of aspiration is said to be the companion of bodhichitta it's it's together with bodhichitta the first one is causal gives rise to bodhichitta the second type of aspiration is a concomitant is the term used. When there's a main mind. And a mental factor together at the same time you say they are concomitant because bodhichitta is actually not a mental factor. But a main mind. Or a primary mind a mental mental consciousness a primary mental consciousness i never heard an explanation as to why that is the case. But everybody says it instead of whatever setting you don't see they don't seem to give a reason for it they just say that's how it is bodhichitta is a primary mind. And then it's accompanied by well probably many mental factors. But one of the main mental factors is this the second one aspiration for complete enlightenment. And there's actually a debate about these two desires. Or aspirations do they both accompany bodhichitta are both of them present together with bodhichitta. Or is the first one just the cause. And the second one is just accompanying it. And apparently there are different opinions. So some llamas say yes both of these two aspirations are there in the mind together with bodhichitta concominant. But others say no no only the second one is present with bodhichitta the first one is just causal. But i don't know all the details of that debate they have their reasons for why they say what they say they probably go into great detail. And get very excited. And have very lively debates about it. But it's a point of debate. And so so these two lines from matreya's text ornament clear relation realization is just a very short explanation of generated mind. And then jetson chooky gelson's text for example 70 topics his text on the 70 topics gives a much more detailed definition. So let's look at that it's on the next slide. So this is his definition of the mahayana conventional oops here it has mind generation that's that's another way of translating generated mind. So i forgot to change that generated mind okay. So i put different colors because there's different parts of the definition that have different meanings. So it's a mahayana special main mental knower that arises concomitant with an assisting aspiration observing complete enlightenment for others welfare. And is distinguished by abiding in a class of paths that serves as the door of entry into mahayana paths. So it's a lot of words there. And. But apparently this is just a very precise definition that would hold up on the debate ground because if you just gave those two lines from matreya's text you might get smashed in a debate. So they really try to you know make sure that definitions are very precise. So the the first term mahayana saying that it's mahayana this eliminates contrived bodhichitta. So remember before you have uncontrived spontaneous bodhichitta you have contrived bodhichitta. And that's. When you have to make effort to generate that state of mind that it's not spontaneous. And naturally arising. And so that kind of bodhichitta contributed isn't genuine buddy cheetah it's more like fake it till you make it i mean it's certainly good it's it's a very good state of mind. But bodhichitta really is the uncontrived natural spontaneous effortless bodhichitta. So putting the term mahayana there eliminates contrived bodhichitta because if you still have just contrived bodhichitta you haven't really entered the mahayana path you only enter the mahayana path. And become a mahayana path person by developing uncontrived bodhichitta. Or generated mind. And then there's the part the next few words in green special main mental knower. So this means it's a main mind rather than a mental factor it's a primary mind a main mind. And it's a mental nowhere nowhere is just another term for mind. And it's special because it's one of the principal states of mind that we need to attain enlightenment i mean we have lots of main minds. But most of them probably don't help us reach enlightenment maybe many of them may help us dance i'm sorry if they are involved with attachment. And anger. And so forth. So this is a very special main mind. And then the next the part in blue is talking about this aspiration. So it arises common concomitant means together with an assisting aspiration observing complete enlightenment for others welfare. So that's talking about the aspiration that is together with bodhichitta looking at enlightenment wanting to achieve enlightenment to be able to benefit others. Then the last phrase that's in kind of orange abiding in a class of paths that serves as the door of entry into mahayana paths. So bodhichitta is called the door of entry into the mahayana path it's because it's. When you generate uncontrived spontaneous bodhichitta that's. When you you're through the door you're in the door you're on the path officially you are part of your part of the mahayana path. And it said that. When you have your first experience of uncontrived bodhichitta. Or generated mind that's the point at which you attain the small level of the path of accumulation that's the first very first level of that path. And then later as you continue on the path you continue having this mind of gen of bodhichitta generated mine in fact it said that a bodhi a bodhisattva is never without bodhichitta in the mind of a bodhisattva there's always some kind of bodhichitta even i guess even. When they're asleep always always has bodhichitta. But we'll have a little bit more about that later. So the bodhichittas that a bodhisattva has later in the path are not the door of entry to the mahayana path it's only that first mind initial experience of uncontrived bodhichitta that's the door of entry. But we can still say that those other levels of bodhichitta that they have later on on the on the later paths they are still in the class of paths there's still that same type of mind that is the door of entry to the mahayana path. So that's the meaning of those all those words at the last part of the definition. So don't worry you know you don't have to memorize this unless you want to. But just yeah this this definition gives more information about what is bodhichitta what is the generated mind. So the next slide is yeah. So there's a lot of information about bodhichitta in the ornament that isn't found in other texts that i have come across. So for example this one who can generate bodhichitta what kind of person what kind of being can generate bodhichitta. And so it talks about two aspects of the of of a being one is the body the kind of body you have body they call it body support. And this is any of the six types of migrators it's interesting. So the six types of migrators are hell beings hungry ghosts animals humans asuras. And davis. So according to this text any of those beings is able to generate bodhichitta. And you may have heard it said they they talk about the buddha shakyamuni buddha. And that. When he first generated bodhichitta he was in hell he was a hell being. And there was some story about him having to pull some big heavy cart. And there was a companion both of them were pulling this big heavy cart. And there was some kind of hell being that was beating them.And the buddha. When he wasn't booted then. But this buddha to be felt compassion for his companion. And he asked can i carry this by myself. And let this person go. So he had that compassion for this other being. And then i think the story was he died. And maybe the hell guardian hit him over the head. Or something. And then he died. And he was out of hell with a great

great thought of compassion that he had. And enabled him to escape from hell. So they do say that that was the first time he generated bodhichitta. But apparently there's debate about that as well [Laughter] yeah some say he didn't really generate bodhichitta at that point in time he generated great compassion because it yeah kind of hard to really generate bodhichitta in the hell in the hell realm because the second point is the mind support the kind of mind you need to have to generate bodhichitta. And it said that it has to be either a preparation of a concentration i.e at least calm abiding. Or an actual concentration. So you're probably familiar with coma biting this is where you train your mind to stay focused on an object for longer. And longer periods of time. And eventually you get to where you can stay focused on your objective meditation for at least four hours without getting tired. Or restless. Or having any faults. And so that's the point at which you have calm abiding. And there's physical. And mental bliss. And pliancy. And so on. And so forth. So it's a very high level of concentration. And then on top of that after developing coma biting you can go on to develop concentrations. Or jhanas i think it's a hollywood gianna in sanskrit. So there are four concentrations these are higher levels of of of mental stability concentration this is a whole complicated explanation of how you do this. But anyway it said that to develop bodhichitta you need to have at least a preparation that's like a step towards a concentration there's seven preparations the first one is calm abiding that's like the first step towards developing a concentration. So you have to at least have attained that. Or an actual concentration. So that's a very high level of mind. And if that's what you need to be able to develop bodhichitta. Then how is it possible for an animal. Or a hungry ghost. Or someone in the hell to be able to have that kind of mind. So i think that's again a topic of debate especially with regard to the story about the buddha. And so those who say that the buddha did generate bodhichitta. When he was in hell that he must have had developed a preparation of a concentration. Or concentration in a past life. And was still still had it in this lifetime which is possible because you know we do hear stories about people human beings for example in this world who very easily very quickly develop concentration calm abiding jhanas. And some have clairvoyance they're able to see other people's minds. Or see things far away that you know they shouldn't be able to see. So there are people who have these kind of abilities. And it's possible that yeah they developed concentration very high concentration in their past life. And they have you know the continuation of that mind even in this lifetime it was possible that buddha was in hell. And he still had this powerful mind from a previous life. And on the basis of that was able to generate bodhichitta. But anyway i guess what we can learn from this is that we do need to develop concentration we need we do need to work on common biting if we want to develop bodhichitta we have to have that as a basis okay. Then there's some different ways of dividing bodhichitta the next slide wishing. And engaging bodhichitta you probably encountered these terms before. So wishing bodhichitta. Or generated mind is the mind wishing to become a buddha to benefit all sentient beings. And so that is compared to having the interest to go someplace to make a journey to some destination like tibet. Or india you know. So you're at home. And you hear about this wonderful place. And you generate this wish i want to go there i want to have that experience of being in that place. But you're not yet doing anything about it. Or just dreaming maybe looking at travel brochures. And so on but. And then the second type of bodhichitta is engaging again i put the wrong letters it should be gm generated mind engaging generated mind. So in general this is the type of bodhichitta that you have. When you're engaging in bodhisattva deeds. When you're actually doing something just like if you finally decide to make that journey. And go to that destination. Then you start planning buying your air ticket. And getting your visa. And packing your bags. And And so on. So you're actually involved in doing what you need to do to get to your destination. And so for the bodhisattva. When they go beyond just wishing to reach enlightenment. And they start doing the practices which are mainly the six perfections giving ethics. And so on. And they're actually engaged in those practices the bodhichitta they have at that time is the second one engaging bodhichitta so. When you first generate bodhichitta the third bullet point. When one first generates bodhichitta it's wishing bodhichita. And then. When we start engaging in the bodhisattva deeds. Then we have engaging bodhichitta. And what it said in the ornament in its commentaries the last bullet point these two types of bodhichitta are mutually exclusive they are not the same not the same thing. And they also cannot both be in the mind at the same time only one of these can be in the mind at the same time. But they are part of a single stream. Or continuity of again i use it i was rushing today it should be generated mind. Or bodhichitta. So from the time that one becomes a bodhisattva having generated spontaneous uncontrived bodhichitta from that time on a bodhisattva always has bodhichitta in their mind. And it's either wishing buddy cheetah. Or engaging bodhichitta one of those two types of bodhichitta is always there in their mind. And the next slide has a bit more about engaging bodhichitta because it's a little bit complicated how this how that works. And so this is from the commentaries to the ornament first bullet point says a bodhisattva has engaging bodhichitta. When two things are manifest the first one is bodhichitta. Or generated mind. So that's manifest. And the meaning of manifest our teacher said is that the person is directly thinking about it it's kind of on the surface of their mind rather than unconscious. Or subliminal. Or you know deeper down in the mind. So it's on the conscious level the surface of their mind. So bodhichitta is manifest. And the second thing that's manifest is the bodhisattva is actively practicing bodhisattvas deeds. So they're practicing giving. Or ethics. Or a combination i mean actually a bodhisattva. When they practice any of the six perfections they practice all six together that's actually one of the later topics in chapter one it's called achieving of armor. And yeah it talks about how. When a bodhisattva is practicing giving at the same time they're practicing ethics patience joy suffered concentration. And wisdom. And when they're practicing joyous effort they're also practicing giving. And And so on. So all six perfections are practiced together in one kind of package yeah. So so. When a bodhisattva is actively engaging in bodhisattvadees like the six perfections. So that's manifest. And their bodhichitta is manifest not subliminal that's the meaning of engaging bodhichitta that's the time. When they have engaging bodhichitta now. So the second bullet points us just an example. When a bodhisattva is practicing giving. And both of those two factors are manifest. Then her bodhichitta her generated mind is engaging engaging generated mind the reason it sometimes says mind generation is that's the term jeffrey uses i think. And i like it. So i was using that for a long time. But. Then the translator sugi she used generated mind. So i was trying to kind of conform to her i still like my generation anyway just another way of translating the term. But. Then bullet point number three this is a tricky one. But during meditative equipoise on emptiness generated mind is non-manifest the reason for that is. So this is talking about because bodhisattvas you know sometimes they sit down. And meditate on emptiness they need to do that they've already realized emptiness. But they need to continue meditating on emptiness. And making their mind more. And more familiar with emptiness. And. And if it's if it's an aria bodhisattva. And they have a direct realization of emptiness then. When they're meditating on emptiness the only thing that appears to their mind is emptiness nothing else besides emptiness appears that means all conventional phenomena all conventional things are just not appearing to their mind sentient beings are not appearing to their mind even their own body. And mind their own self isn't appearing to their mind nothing except emptiness is appearing to their mind. And so that's why it said that generated mind. Or bodhichitta is not manifest at that time because for that to be manifest the bodhisattva has to be thinking about sentient beings. And thinking about enlightenment. And wanting to reach enlightenment to help sinning beings. And they're not doing that at that time because those things none of those things are appearing in their mind the only thing appearing is emptiness. And so so. When they're in meditative poison emptiness their bodhichitta goes subliminal goes underground this is according to jetson chookie gelson. But apparently there are different opinions about this [Music] for example. When master panchan sanandrappa another writer of textbooks he doesn't agree that there's such a thing as a non-manifest mind. So i don't know how he explains this. But but anyway since i've my teachers follow jetson tsuki gelton that i've learned. So it's they just say yeah bodhichitta goes non-manifest it goes subliminal it's still there in the mind it's still present in the mind. But it's not manifest it can't be manifest because nothing appears except emptiness. And so. When the generated mind the bodhichitta becomes not a manifest it's wishing bodhichitta yeah because because to for buddy for in order to have engaging body cheat it has to be manifest. When it's not manifest it turns into wishing buddhi cheetah. And so even though this bodhisattva is engaging in the bodhisattva deeds at that moment because they're meditating on emptiness. And that's one of the bodhisattva deeds it's a sixth perfection. So they are actively engaging in the bodhisattva deeds at that moment however because their bodhichitta is not manifest it can't be engaging bodhichitta it's wishing cheetah does that make sense it's a little tricky. But again there's probably different points of view different assertions about this explanations about. But this. But this is according to justin chooky gelson. And to me it's yeah sounds good makes sense. And then yeah. So the last bullet point just kind of repeats engaging bodhichitta must always be manifest okay whereas wishing bodhichitta can be manifest. Or non-manifest because in the beginning. When you first generate bodhichitta it's wishing bodhichitta. And it's manifest. And then. When you start engaging in bodhisattva deeds practicing giving. And ethics. And so on. And so forth. Then you can have engaging buddhi cheetah. But. When engaging bodhichitta has to become non-manifest like during meditative equipoise it can no longer be engaging bodhichitta. So it's wishing bodhichitta. So there's always bodhichitta in the mind sometimes it's engaging buddhi cheetah sometimes it's wishing. So if you don't understand that don't worry [Laughter] what you need to understand is that yeah there are these two types of bodhichitta we need to cultivate. And so we need to engage in the various meditation practices to cultivate this aspiration to become a buddha to benefit all living beings okay. So the next point is kind of fun does a buddha have bodhichitta. So again it seems there are different opinions about this different tibetan scholars. And writers of texts will give different opinions about it it seems that they are unanimous that a buddha doesn't have wishing bodhichitta i suppose one reason for that is because wishing bodhichittas i want to become enlightened. And they're already there okay. So they no longer need to have the wish to become enlightened. But another reason is that a buddha is always engaged in actively working to help sentient beings i guess you wouldn't call it bodhisattva deeds anymore they would be buddha deeds rather than bodhisattva deeds. But anyway a buddha is constantly actively working for sentient beings helping sentient beings. And so whatever bodhichitta they have would be engaging bodhichitta however some scholars say no a buddha doesn't have even engaging buddhi cheetah. And their reason is because bodhichitta seeks enlightenment. And that's already been attained yeah. So they think it just sounds weird to say buddha has bodhichitta wanting to become enlightened because he's already there he doesn't need booty cheetah anymore. But. Then on the other hand it sounds kind of uncomfortable to say. But it doesn't have bodhichitta. So some scholars in the third bullet point. And this includes jetson chooky gelsen who wrote the text about the 70 topics they. So they say that buddha does have engaging bodhichitta. And they say that. So again engaging bodhichitta has the aspiration for enlightenment. So they say a buddha seeks enlightenment not for himself. But for others. So is he is seeking enlightenment aspiring for enlightenment for other people other beings. Or all sentient beings. So from that point of view they say it is okay to say that a buddha has bodhichitta don't know for me that seems like a nice way around the problem i just wouldn't feel comfortable with the thing. But it doesn't have. But i can see the point it does sound a bit strange if you define bodhichitta as the aspiration to reach enlightenment well once you're there you still need that mind okay. So. Then another next slide is another way of dividing bodhichitta. And these this is into conventional body cheetah. And ultimate bodhichitta. So you may have heard those terms conventional bodhichitta ultimate bodhichitta. But in fact this isn't a real division of bodhichitta it's just terminological it's just a name only because ultimate bodhichitta is not really bodhichitta it's kind of tricky they call it you know they talk about ultimate bodhichitta. But. When you examine what exactly is ultimate bodhichitta it's not bodhichitta. But i guess we do have examples of that calling you know giving a certain name. Or term to something even though it's not that. So we do that in english. And they do it in tibetan. And sanskrit as well. So what is okay. So first let's look at conventional buddhi cheetah. So conventional bodhichitta is what we've been talking about all along the aspiration to become a buddha to become fully awakened for the benefit of all sentient beings. So that's a conventional buddhi cheetah. And it's in it exists from the mahayana path of accumulation through ground. So buddha ground that term buddha ground just means yeah. When you're at the level of a buddha. When you have the mind of a buddha. So according yeah according to this explanation. Then even on the buddha ground buddhists still exist it's still there yeah. So wishing bodhichitta engaging bodhichitta those are both conventional bodhichitta now ultimate bodhichitta the third bullet point is this is a definition. So it's a little technical a mahayana arya's main mental knower that directly realizes the emptiness of true existence of enlightenment okay. So if we break that down unpack that ultimate bodhichitta saying that it's mahayana means it's only in the mind of a bodhisattva only bodhisattvas have ultimate bodhichitta. And it has to be a mahayana arya that's a person who has directly realized emptiness. So only mahayana aryas have ultimate bodhichitta. And it's a main mental knower it's a primary mind that directly realizes the emptiness of true existence of enlightenment. So it's wisdom basically wisdom directly realizing emptiness. And it mentions specifically the emptiness of enlightenment. And my teacher said the reason that it specifies enlightenment because actually a direct realization of emptiness realizes the emptiness of all phenomena even though to start with maybe you were just meditating on one object like your own eye. Or your mind. Or your body. Or whatever. So you was using that object to meditate on. And realize emptiness. But then. When you have the direct realization of emptiness. When you see emptiness directly non-conceptually you are realizing the emptiness of all phenomena the emptiness of true existence of everything all phenomena. So this mind doesn't only realize the emptiness of enlightenment it realizes emptiness of all phenomena. But the reason it specifies the emptiness of true existence of enlightenment our teacher says it's because you know we're talking about ultimate bodhichitta the term ultimate bodhichitta. And since we say ultimate bodhichitta. Or mind of enlightenment bodhichitta means mind of enlightenment. Then you you have to say the term ultimate. And enlightenment. So it's realizing the ultimate nature the ultimate nature the final mode of existence of enlightenment anyway he explained that's the reason that it the definition is given in this way. So that's why ultimate bodhichitta isn't really bodhichitta because it isn't the wish to become enlightened it's the wisdom realizing the emptiness of inherent existence of enlightenment as well as all other phenomena. And the next bullet point says ultimate bodhichitta is free of the three types of dualistic appearances. So the three types of dualistic appearances actually there's more than three. But the main ones are one type is appearance of true existence. So for us ordinary beings who haven't realized emptiness things appear truly existing we have the appearance of true existence whatever we think about our body our mind our eye other people other beings buddha enlightenment all the things we perceive appear truly existing as the appearance of true existence where whereas. When a person is in meditation meditative equipoise directly realizing emptiness there's no appearance of true existence all appearances of true existence have vanished. And in fact that's really the first time ever in your whole existence from beginningless time that true existence disappears. So until that point there's always going to be appearances of true existence. So it must be pretty amazing. So that's one type of dualistic appearance. And another type is the appearances of conventionalities just conventional things like bodies. And tables. And chairs. And cats. And dogs. And mountains. And trees. So everything that isn't emptiness is a conventionality. So all of those things disappear as well they don't appear. When your mind is in that meditation directly realizing emptiness that's another kind of dualistic appearance. And then the third type of dualistic appearance is the appearance of subject. And object as different entities. So normally. When we have an experience seeing hearing thinking. And so on there's this sense of a subject over here. And an object over there over there you know like two separate things. And in fact there are two separate things subject to an object are not the same. But that's our usual experience. But they say that. When when a person is meditating on emptiness. And having the direct realization of emptiness that sense of a separate subject an object disappears. And they say yeah the sense of a separate subject over here looking at emptiness over there just vanishes stops. And the only thing that appears is emptiness there isn't even a sense of eye. Or mind looking at emptiness perceiving emptiness just emptiness itself. So they say it's a sense of an eye. Or a subject kind of flows into emptiness merges with emptiness in the same way that if you pour a glass of water into a pitcher of water the glass of water will completely mix with the water in the picture. And you can no longer distinguish it they use that analogy to describe this experience of your mind your yourself over here merging with the object emptiness. And just becoming indistinguishable from it. So again it must be a amazing experience to have. So yeah. So those are three types of dualistic appearances that disappear don't appear. When an aria is meditating on. And having a direct realization of emptiness. So this is another meaning of nonduality that term nonduality that came up earlier you know talking about the the more cheetah matra point of view of subject. And object arising from the same seed in the mind that's one meaning of nonduality. But this is another meaning of nonduality absence of duality dualistic appearances. So you have to be careful with that term nonduality because it's used in different contexts. And has different meanings. So some people just kind of blah blah blah about nonduality. But you have to check what do you mean by nonduality what kind of nonduality are you talking about don't just assume that we all understand that word in the same way. And the last bullet point says conventional. And ultimate bodhichitta represent method. And wisdom. So you probably heard this saying about how a bodhisattva needs these two wings just like a bird needs two wings to fly a bodhisattva needs two wings of method. And wisdom to fly to enlightenment. So conventional bodhichitta is like the method side of the path. And then ultimate bodhichitta is the wisdom side. So bodhisattva needs to cultivate practice both of those to reach enlightenment we just have a little bit more. And i would like to finish this topic of bodhichitta this time. So we can do something else next time. So in the ornament there's also an explanation of well it's not really an explanation it's just a list of 22 kinds of bodhichitta. So i'll just show the next slide i'm not going to go into all of these. But just for auspiciousness there are 22 types of bodhichitta. And so matreya just mentions their names no explanation at all. So that shows how important it is to have commentaries. So the names of the 22 bodhichittas are earth gold moon fire meaning there's er bodhichitta that's like the earth bodhichitta that's like gold bodhichitta that's like the moon bodhichitta that's like fire. And so on like treasure like a jewel mine like an ocean like a vajra like mountain like medicine like a spiritual guide wish granting gem sun song king treasury highway mount geyser pleasant sound river. And cloud. So those are the 22 types of bodhichitta. And then in the commentaries it explains a bit more because these different types of bodhichitta occur at different points of the path. So the first one the earth-like bodhichitta is the first bodhichitta that is developed the first uncontrived bodhichitta it's called like the earth. And the reason it's called like that is because just as the earth is the basis for growing crops. And building buildings. So everything depends on the earth we didn't have the earth we wouldn't be able to have all of these things. So in the same way this this type of bodhichitta the first kind of bodhichitta bodhisattva develops is the basis of all wholesome qualities the basis of all good things yeah. So there are books sources where you can get more information probably one of the volumes of volume i'm not sure yeah one of the volumes of the library of wisdom. And compassion by venerable children. And nice holiness the dalai lama listen to these okay one more one last slide. And this isn't really mentioned in matreya's text ornament. But it's in the commentaries. And you've probably heard it before three ways that bodhichitta is generated it's like those who are generating bodhichitta aspiring for enlightenment they have three different sort of attitudes. Or ways of thinking how they're going to reach enlightenment. And help sentient beings. And so the first one is is king-like. So that's having the kind of thought like i will achieve enlightenment first. And then i will lead all sentient beings to that state. So i will be like the leader like a king leading all sentient beings to enlightenment. So that's one way of thinking about it the second one is boatman-like. Or captain like. So this is thinking all sentient beings. And i will intake will attain enlightenment together. So it's like you imagine yourself like a captain of a boat a ship. And all sending beings are on board. And you're all going to enlightenment together. And the third is like a herdsman like a shepherd you know the way a shepherd relates to their sheep they kind of drive the sheep ahead of them. And they they're in in the back probably to make sure nobody goes astray nobody gets left behind. So they're kind of hurting the sheep in front of them. So this

this way of thinking is i will place all sentient beings in the state of enlightenment. And then i will attain enlightenment. So i'll be the last one there yeah. So my teacher said these three modes depend on the mental strength of the trainees those who have great mental strength like the sharp faculty bodhisattvas they are like the third one the herdsmen i mean it takes a lot of strength to think that way i will let everyone else reach enlightenment first. And i'll be the last one there yeah. And those with middle strength are like the second one the boatman taking all sending beings along with you to enlightenment. And then those with the least mental strength are like the king the first one wanting to be there first. But in reality they say that even like the third one that hurts the one who wants to get there last it won't happen that way because you have such strong body cheetah. And compassion. And you know concern for others altruism. And so little self-centeredness that even if you're you know kicking. And screaming. And saying no i don't want to reach enlightenment. But it'll happen that's what they say that's anecdotal. But it makes sense yeah okay. So that's as much as i wanted to cover today. So the ornament itself doesn't explain the methods for how to develop woody cheetah. So those are found in the lamrim on other texts for example that well there's two main methods for developing bodhichitta one is the seven fold cause. And effect instruction which well before you even start the seven you you meditate on equanimity to overcome the tendency to relegate beings to these three positions of friend enemy stranger try to even out your feelings towards others. So you stop discriminating. And having biased attitudes towards them. And then the actual seven points start with thinking of all sentient beings as mother they've all been my mother in past lives. And then the second is thinking of their kindness. When they were my mother what did they do for me it brought me into the world. And they cared for me. When i was small. And vulnerable. And and. And so on. And so forth just like our mother of this life. Or just like good mothers everywhere. And so that is to engender a strong sense of affection like if we really appreciate what our mother does for us in this life we feel. So much affection for her. And we're ready to help her we put everything aside. And jump to help her. When she needs help. So if everyone has played that role in our mother. Then we can generate very strong affection for others. And then we go on to think about how to repay their kindness. And we can help them now in this life. But really helping them is by helping them get out of samsara helping them achieve nirvana. And enlightenment. And then we go on to meditate on love a special kind of love wishing sentient beings to be happy to have happiness all the different kinds of happiness up to the highest happiness of enlightenment. And then compassion wishing them to be free of suffering all the different kinds of suffering. So by meditating in all these points again. And again. And again over a long period of time. And you finally get to the point of having what's called a sometimes it's called universal responsibility. Or the extraordinary wish. Or the special thought there's different ways of translating that. So this is where you you you know get what you decide to take on that responsibility of helping sentient beings have happiness. And freedom from suffering. And then that leads to bodhichitta. So realizing that how to help sentient beings the best way to help them the only way to really help them is by becoming a buddha yourself. So. Then you make that your goal set your set your sights on enlightenment with this sense of strong love. And compassion. So those are the main points of that method for developing bodhichitta. So you're probably all familiar with them. But yeah we need to meditate on these points again. And again in order to generate this attitude of bodhichitta. And the other method i'll i'll mention it next week. Or maybe we could do a little bit of meditation we didn't really have time tonight i was talking too much. So next week we can start with some meditation. So we have a few minutes left if anyone has a question you'd like to ask yes does wishing. And engaging only apply to spontaneous bodhichitta. Or could contrive also be divided they don't i don't think they use those terms yeah i think wishing bodhichita engaging bodhichitta those terms are only applied to actual uncontrived voting cheetah. So how would you describe an ordinary being who has this contrived wish. And engages in like generosity of course yeah i mean before we become bodhisattvas before we have real uncontrived we do need to be practicing generosity. And ethics. And so on. And so forth. And we we try our best to have the bodhi cheat of motivation for doing these practices. But it's not yet the real thing you know it's like we're we're dressed maybe dress rehearsal. Or something. And we're rehearsing. But yeah at our level at my level anyway yeah i just try to have the bodhichitta motivation. And try to practice giving. And ethics to the best of my ability. And of course it's valuable. And beneficial. And it's you know creating the causes to eventually have genuine bodhichitta. And be on the bodhisattvas path. And reach enlightenment. But yeah usually in the text. When they talk about bodhichitta it is the uncontrived form because that's. When you really are like. When they talk about accumulating merit for enlightenment the three countless great eons of merit that a bodhisattva on the sutra path needs to cultivate that actually starts from the path of accumulation. So whatever merit we're creating now i mean of course it is it is you know helping us get to enlightenment. But it's not officially part of the accumulation of merit until we have genuine uncontrived body cheetah i hope this doesn't sound discouraging [Laughter] that's how it is anyone from the online students [Music] what's up well. Then i guess we can finish. So we'll dedicate the merit the positive energy of spending this time together learning more about the bodhisattvas practices. And deeds. And hopefully feeling very inspired to learn more. But to practice more. So that one day we can actually be bodhisattvas engaging in bodhisattva deeds. And actually making our way to enlightenment [Music]. So we definitely created merit positive energy by spending this time together looking at this these topics. And the best thing we can do with our merit is to share it with others all living beings they've all been our kind mothers we've received kindness. And help gifts from every single living being. And [Music]. So let's generate the strong wish to repay their kindness benefit them in return. And this is one way we can do that by sharing our merit our positive energy with them let's wish that the merit we've accumulated here tonight will benefit all sentient beings help them all to generate in their own minds these positive thoughts these positive attitudes of love. And compassion. And wisdom. And eventually bodhichitta. So that they can we can all progress together on the path. And ultimately reach full enlightenment buddhahood due to the merits of these virtuous actions may i quickly attain the state of guru buddha. And lead all living beings without exception into that enlightened state may the supreme jewel buddy cheetah that has not arisen arias is real. And may that which has arisen not diminish. But increase more the source of every benefit. And happiness in the world. And may you have a long life. And all your holy wishes be spontaneously fulfilled you who will uphold the subduers who are away who serve as the bountiful bearer of all sustaining preserving. And spreading manjuna's victorious doctrine who masterfully accomplish magnificent prayers honoring the three sublime ones the savior of myself. And others your disciples please please live it wrong we we can also mentally dedicate to the long lives of all spiritual masters. So each of us may have other spiritual masters that we've learned from. And that we value regard as precious. And want them to live a long time. And then spiritual masters of other people. And other beings. So let's dedicate that all teachers who are teaching the genuine teachings of the path to enlightenment may they all live long healthy lives. And may all their wishes. And prayers be fulfilled okay thank you

Made in United States
North Haven, CT
25 January 2024